WORLD STOR
ENCYCLOP

100

AMAZING
FOOTBALL
STORIES

**INTERESTING FOOTBALL FACTS
AND TRIVIA FOR SMART KIDS
AND CURIOUS PEOPLE**

PRESENTATION

THIS BOOK IS PART OF **THE WORLD STORIES ENCYCLOPEDIA** SERIES, AN IMPORTANT PUBLISHING PROJECT SPECIALIZED IN PUBLICATIONS FOR CHILDREN AND YOUNG PEOPLE.

THE SERIES INCLUDES VARIOUS BOOKS WITH A FASCINATING SELECTION OF AMAZING STORIES, FACTS AND CURIOSITIES **ABOUT FOOTBALL, VARIOUS SPORTS, ANIMALS, NATURE, SCIENCE.**

ALL WITH THE HELP AND ADVICE OF EXPERTS IN THE SECTOR TO ALWAYS PROVIDE HIGH-QUALITY INFORMATION AND CONTENT.

WHAT IS EVEN MORE ATTRACTIVE IS THAT THROUGH THESE BOOKS CHILDREN AND YOUNG PEOPLE WILL PERFECT THEIR KNOWLEDGE AND LOGICAL CAPABILITIES SIMPLY HAVING FUN. **WHAT'S MORE BEAUTIFUL?**

GOOD READING AND ENJOY.

1

When everything began…

The first modern football match was officially played in 1860 in England. The first official match saw Sheffield (the first official football club founded in 1857) face Hallam.

The match consisted in a derby, as both teams were from Sheffield. Sheffield won 2-0. The first goal was scored by captain Nathaniel Creswick. In this match the rule of not being able to catch the ball with the hands (fair catch) had not yet been introduced.

2

The Unconventional Goalkeeper

In a small village in the heart of England, there was a football team with a rather unique goalkeeper named Reggie. Reggie was known for his exceptional agility and quick reflexes, but what truly set him apart was his knack for playing in unconventional ways. During one particularly rainy match, Reggie ditched his goalkeeping gloves and opted for bare hands, claiming he could grip the wet ball better. To everyone's amazement, his tactic worked, and the team won the match. Reggie's creative approach to goalkeeping became a local legend, inspiring young players to think outside the box.

3

The Mysterious Streaker

In the midst of a heated rivalry match between two Premier League teams, an unexpected twist occurred that left everyone bewildered.

Midway through the second half, a streaker dashed onto the pitch, interrupting the game. However, this wasn't just any streaker – he had painted his body in the team colors of both clubs, creating a hilarious spectacle. Surprisingly, both sets of fans found themselves laughing together, momentarily putting their rivalry aside.

The streaker's antics brought an unexpected sense of unity to the stadium that day, reminding everyone that football is, after all, a game meant to be enjoyed.

4

The Phantom Whistle

In a lower-league match in Scotland, a peculiar incident unfolded that left players and fans scratching their heads.

During a critical penalty kick, just as the striker was about to make his shot, a distinct whistle echoed through the stadium. The striker hesitated, and the goalkeeper made an easy save. However, both teams were baffled as no one had blown the whistle.

The referee was equally perplexed, but after consulting with his assistants, the goal was disallowed, much to the dismay of the attacking team. To this day, nobody knows where the mysterious whistle sound came from, and it remains one of the most curious moments in football history.

The Altitude Challenge

In Bolivia, football takes on a unique twist due to the country's high altitude. La Paz, the capital city, sits at over 11,900 feet above sea level, creating a challenging environment for visiting teams. The thin air at such altitudes can lead to rapid fatigue, shortness of breath, and even nausea.

Bolivian teams have a distinct home advantage, as their players are acclimated to the conditions. However, visiting teams often struggle, and the matches can produce surprising results.

This geographical quirk adds an extra layer of intrigue to Bolivian football and showcases how diverse factors can influence the beautiful game.

The Superstitious Manager

In the English Championship, there was a manager named Arthur, known for his quirky superstitions. He believed that wearing mismatched socks brought his team good luck, so he'd intentionally choose socks of different colors before every match.

He also insisted on performing a cartwheel onto the pitch before kick-off, convinced it would bring positive energy.

Despite his unconventional beliefs, Arthur led his team to several promotions and even a surprise cup victory. Players who initially found his antics odd eventually embraced his superstitions, recognizing that his unique approach added a touch of charm to their football journey.

7

The Adema v SO Emyrne match holds the record for goals scored in a single match ever. Indeed, AS Adema beat Emyrne 149-0. Both teams came from Antananarivo, the capital of Madagascar.

The match was a derby. As a form of protest, the SO Emyrne coach invited his players to score their own goals, because they were upset by a referee's choice relating to the previous match. From then on it was a frenzy... the fans left the stands asking for a refund of the ticket.

The Emyrne players complained further, finally asking the Adema even to round it up to 150-0!

8

Pelé, the greatest football player of all time, was declared a "National Treasure" by the President of Brazil Jânio Quadros and also a "Historical Heritage of Humanity" in 2011.
Furthermore, his name is part of the "National Football Hall of Fame", an American football museum born with the intention of paying homage to those who have contributed most to improving the image of the USA in football in the world.

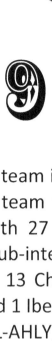

9

The most successful team in the world is REAL MADRID, a Spanish team from the capital of the same name, with 27 international titles won, including 7 club-intercontinental world titles, 2 UEFA Cups, 13 Champions League, 4 UEFA Super Cups and 1 Ibero-American Cup.

In second place is AL-AHLY, an Egyptian sports club based in the city of Cairo, with 21 trophies and in third place is an Italian team, Milan, with 18 trophies.

10

The "Golden Ball" is one of the most prestigious and eagerly awaited awards in the world of football, it is awarded annually to the best player of the year and creates strong anticipation among fans.

With an expert jury from French and international newspapers voting for the winner, the final choice is always at the center of discussion and debate. The award represents a prestigious recognition for a footballer's career and remains one of the most exciting events of the football season.

11

The most successful football team in Italy is Juventus, with 70 titles. 36 championships, 14 Italian Cups and 9 Italian Super Cups, 2 Champions Leagues, 3 UEFA Cups. Milan is in second place, with 49 total trophies, including 19 scudetti, 7 Champions Leagues, 5 Italian Cups and 7 Italian Super Cups. In third place is Inter, with 42 titles, including 19 scudetti, 6 Italian Super Cup, 7 Italian Cup, 3 Champions League.

12

The "treble" in Italy is held by Inter. The treble is a recognition given to a football team that wins the 3 most important tournaments in the same season. In Italy, to win the treble, you need to win the championship, the national cup and the Champions League at the same time.

The treble in England is held by Manchester United, in Spain by Barcelona and in Germany by Bayern Munich.

13

It might seem absurd, but Pelé (for many the strongest player of all time) managed to stop a war for a couple of days.

It happened in 1967, at the time when a real civil war called "Biafra War" was taking place in Nigeria

This was cut short for two days as people had to see Pele play football.

At that moment the Brazilian was playing a tournament with Santos in Nigeria.

In 2013, Cristiano Ronaldo, Portuguese footballer and captain of his national team set a personal best by scoring 69 goals in 59 games. This allowed him to become the first player in history to surpass the threshold of 61 goals scored in a single season, setting a new standard of excellence in the world of football. In addition, Cristiano Ronaldo has won 5 Ballons d'Or and other awards. These achievements demonstrate Cristiano Ronaldo's extraordinary ability and determination, making him one of the greatest footballers of all time.

15

The stripes of the football field are different to make the viewing experience of the spectators more pleasant. The interesting thing is how this particular effect is achieved.

The blades of grass are bent in one direction or the other, when the threads are bent in the direction of the spectators, the grass appears darker in color, because only the tips are seen and they reflect less light, in the other direction instead the surface is greater, therefore the grass, reflecting more light, appears lighter.

16

The goalkeeper's uniform is the only shirt that is different from that of the other players, this is to distinguish him better. A different shirt facilitates the task of referees and assistants when he leaves the area to try to block an attack in advance.

The goalkeepers of the two teams cannot have the same shirt. If the shirt is the same, the goalkeeper of the home team hosting the opposing team will have to change shirt before entering the field. This decision is supported by the referee.

17

The game ball hasn't changed in 120 years either in shape or size. Ironically, the players of the past would be perfectly capable of using a modern ball.

Changing a ball, in terms of weight, shape or size today would mean having to relearn the game of football, as football players are trained to calibrate their shots on the basis of the modern ball.

18

In many parts of the world, football is called "Football"... however, in the United States, Canada and Australia, the sport is known as "Football". The difference in denomination derives from the different history and sporting tradition of these countries.

In America and Canada, American football is very popular and influential, while in the rest of the world, football reigns supreme. The name "Football" was therefore adopted to avoid confusion between the two different sports.

19

Cristiano Ronaldo, one of the most talented and acclaimed players in the history of football, has a surprising curiosity related to his physique. Ronaldo would have a very different smell which distinguishes him from other players.

This characteristic would be attributed to his balanced diet and his exceptional physical shape. To date, Ronaldo also has his own line of perfumes, branded "CR7".

20

Cristiano Ronaldo follows an extremely strict diet to maintain his exceptional fitness. He eats 6 meals a day. Every 3 hours. He doesn't drink coke or sodas. He doesn't drink alcohol. Do not eat sweets, foods with a lot of sugar or junk food. Don't magic pasta.

He eats mainly lean proteins, such as fish and chicken. Ronaldo consumes only whole foods and drinks plenty of water to keep his body hydrated. This strict diet allows him to maintain optimal physical shape and prevent injuries, allowing him to continue playing at an exceptional level even at an advanced age for the world of football.

21

Cristiano Ronaldo is known for his extraordinary athletic skills. He shoots real "missiles" up to 117 km/h (his running speed reaches around 39 km/h, an agility which allows him to change direction in a tenth of a second and a strength in jumping and head that allows him to jump up to 2.78 meters). These numerical quantities prove that he is a highly versatile player and a terrible threat to any opposing team. His dedication to training and these physical characteristics make him a role model for athletes around the world.

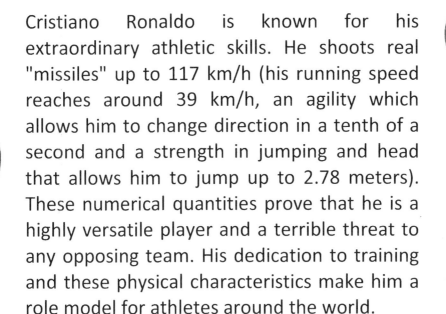

22

The most powerful shot in football history was performed by Ronny Heberson in 2007. His shot reached a speed of 221 km/h, setting a record that still stands today. Heberson was playing for Naval at the time and the match was played against Sporting Lisbon. In the video, the "torpedo" is so fast that it is barely tracked by the cameras, it was a shot taken from a free-kick and subsequently went viral.

23

The first football match broadcast on Italian TV was played on February 5, 1950. The match was Milan against Juventus, won by Milan 7-1 against Juventus, by the Swedish trio Gren-Nordahl-Liedholm.

The match took place at the municipal stadium in Turin. The first ever TV game in history took place on April 9, 1938. It was broadcast by the English channel BBC. It was an inter-British tournament between England and Scotland. The match ended 1-0 for Scotland.

24

In the ranking of the 10 best players of all time there are: in 1st place, Pele (Brazil), in 2nd place Maradona (Argentina), in 3rd place Michel Platini (France), in 4th Johan Cruyff (Holland), in 5th Franz Anton Beckenbauer (Germany), 6th Cristiano Ronaldo (Portugal), 7th Lionel Messi (Argentina), 8th Zinedine Zidane (France), 9th Alfredo di Stefano (Argentina) and 10th Marco Van Basten (Holland), tied with Ferenc Puskas (Hungary).

25

The 5 best teams with the greatest economic value in the world, the ranking. In 1st place is Real Madrid (Spain) with $5.1 billion, tied with Barcelona (Spain). In second place is Manchester United (England) with 4.6 billion dollars. In third place is Liverpool (England) with 4.45 billion. In fourth place Bayern Munich (Germany) - 4.3 billion. In fifth place Manchester City (England) - 4.2 billion. In 9th place is an Italian team, Juventus, with $2.45 billion.

26

The ranking of the most popular teams in the world is as follows: in first place is Manchester United (England) with 650 million fans worldwide, in second place Barcelona (Spain), with 450 million fans, in third Real Madrid Madrid (Spain) with 350 million fans.

Chelsea (England) in fourth with 145 million and Arsenal (England) in fifth with 125 million. On the 8th and 9th floor there are two Italian teams. Respectively, Milan with 95 million fans worldwide and Inter with 55 million.

27

In June 1994 Andrés Escobar - defender of Atlético Nacional, was assassinated. Andrés scored an own goal in the match against the USA, which cost Colombia the elimination from the football world cup.

He was shot dead with six machine-gun shots in a bar parking lot shortly after being repatriated. It is thought that the motive for the murder was the large losses suffered in clandestine bets due to the own goal committed by the unfortunate defender.

28

The continent with the most football players is Asia with 85 million players, followed by Europe with 62 million, Africa - 46 million, North America - 43 million, South America 27 million and Oceania 0.5 million. players. The estimate is based on statistics that consider the number of members of football clubs.

29

Ronaldo, at the 1996 Atlanta Olympics, during the Brazil – Hungary match, would have taken advantage of a moment of confusion to urinate on the pitch. To help himself he would have used the ball, while he was on his knees while the match was stopped. This information would be confirmed by himself a little later.

30

The shirt of the Italian national team is blue because the color derives from the noble coat of arms of the House of Savoy. The first match in the blue shirt was played on January 6, 1911 against Hungary, as a tribute to the royal family. At the beginning, a year earlier, instead of the "savoy blue" there were white shirts. The debut took place on May 15, 1910 in Milan, a year earlier against France, the first match ever played by Italy.

31

The very first footballers who made their debut for the Italian national football team on May 15, 1910 did not look like professional footballers at all, they were football amateurs, they had neither the physique nor the athletic preparation of modern footballers. By profession they did something else altogether: they were university students, accountants and mechanics.

32

In 1927 Benito Mussolini had a new symbol affixed next to the Savoy cross on the old shirts of the Italian national team: the fasces. Furthermore, the national team was forced to change the color of the shirts to black instead of blue as fascist propaganda. Players were also required to salute at the start of each game with the Roman salute.

33

The numerical record of the Golden Balls is held by the Argentine (captain of his national team) Lionel Andrés Messi Cuccittini. "Leo Messi" is a midfielder and striker for Paris Saint-Germain and the Argentina national team. Follows Messi, in second place, with 5 titles Cristiano Ronaldo dos Santos Aveiro. Cristiano Ronaldo is the Portuguese striker of Al-Nassr, one of the most titled clubs in Arabia. In third place, with 3 titles, is Michel Platini, a former French footballer. Platini was an undisputed star in the world of football in the years between the 70s and 80s.

34

The number 1 behind the shirt uniquely identifies the goalkeeper, an attacker cannot wear the number 1. Once upon a time, the number 9 was assigned by tradition, the numbers from 2 to 5 were assigned to the defence, 6 and 8 to the midfielders and 10 to the player who created the most tempting chances on the opponent's ¾. 11 and 12, on the other hand, were the numbers assigned to the fast and more technical forwards who travel on the flanks.

Today the assignment (apart from the goalkeeper's number 1) is no longer so rigid, for example a striker could also wear the number 7 shirt.

35

Kazuyoshi Miura, known as Kazu is a Japanese footballer, striker of the Suzuka Point Getters. At 55, he is officially the oldest player in the history of professional football. In Italy the scepter is held by Gianluigi Buffon, with his respectable 44 years. Buffon is goalkeeper and captain of Parma, which among other things also holds third place in the world, immediately after Vitorino Hilton, a Brazilian footballer currently active in the French third division (Sète).

36

Lionel Messi has Italian ancestry. He is the son of a steel mill worker and Celia María Cuccittini, a cleaning lady. His paternal great-great-grandfather (Angelo Messi) migrated from Recanati (a small town in the province of Macerata in the Marche region) in 1883.

His maternal great-great-grandfather Raniero Coccettini instead migrated back in 1899. Furthermore, Messi would also appear to be a relative (a distant descendant) of the former boxer Italian Luca Messi, with whom he shares family origins.

37

In Japan they have built a football field on the roof of the Tokyo skyscraper. The field is unique of its kind and has a fantastic view, it is called "Adidas Futsal Park Shibuia", the stadium is actually an a5 football field, but in any case you can enjoy a spectacular panorama at night: giant screens and the view of the Tokyo by night.

38

Henningsvaer Stadion is a peculiar football ground located in Norway in the village of Lofoten Islands, off the northern coast. It is considered one of the most beautiful stadiums in the world, precisely because it overlooks the splendid Norwegian Sea and is close to the Arctic Circle. It has no stands or grandstands, and is surrounded only by wild Norwegian nature.

39

In a match between West Ham and Newcastle, Alvin Martin scored a hat-trick against three different Newcastle goalkeepers all in the same match.

The match finished 8-1 and to this day this record remains one of a kind.

40

Historic Florentine football is a medieval sport in vogue in the 1500s and could be considered an ancient predecessor of football. In reality, historic Florentine football has only the word "calcio" and the ball in common with football (which the players can hold in their hands). This sport is very different from football in rules (apart from the goal of goals into the net), it could at best be seen as a mix between a combat sport and rugby. In historic Florentine football almost everything is allowed: tackles, immobilizations, empty hand boxing and even hand-to-hand combat.

41

In 1955 the Champions Cup was born. It is the most important tournament in Europe. The winning teams of their respective national championships participate. The first 5 editions, from 1956 to 1960 were won by Real Madrid. Real Madrid is also the team that has won the most European Cups ever. In 1992 the "Coppa Dei Campioni" changed its name and became the "UEFA Champions League".

42

The UEFA Champions League is Europe's premier football club competition. The most interesting aspect is the group stage and its classification criteria. 32 teams face each other divided into 4 pots: A,B,C,D. The objective of the teams during the groups is to finish in the top 2, to advance to the next stage of the tournament. The final position in the table is determined by the total number of points obtained during the group matches.

43

The ranking of the teams with the most wins in the history of the UEFA Champions League (formerly known as the European Champion Clubs' Cup) is as follows: Real Madrid: 13 wins, AC Milan: 7 wins, Bayern Munich: 6 wins, Liverpool : 6 wins, Barcelona: 5 wins, Ajax: 4 wins, Inter Milan: 3 wins, Manchester United: 3 wins, Juventus: 2 wins, Benfica: 2 wins.

44

The 15 most important competitions in the world are: UEFA Champions League (Europe), UEFA Europa League (Europe), Copa Libertadores (Latin America), FIFA World Cup (world), UEFA European Championship (Europe), African Cup of Nations (Africa), AFC Asian Cup (Asia), Copa America (Latin America), OFC Nations Cup (Oceania), CAF Champions League (Africa), AFC Champions League (Asia), A-League (Australia), Serie A (Italy) , La Liga (Spain), Bundesliga (Germany).

45

The UEFA Europa League (UEFA EURO) is another European-level football competition, which is organized annually by the European Football Union (UEFA). This competition includes teams that have not participated in the UEFA Champions League or have not reached the next stage of the Champions League, so it is a second chance for the teams to be able to compete at European level.

46

The Copa Libertadores is a football competition organized by CONMEBOL for South American football clubs. It is considered the most important and prestigious football competition in Latin America and features teams from 10 South American countries. It begins with a group stage and is followed by a knockout stage. The winning team is awarded the title of "Latin American champion" and has the opportunity to participate in the Intercontinental Cup. The Copa Libertadores attracts football fans and enthusiasts from all over the world.

47

The Italian Football Championship, known as Serie A, is an annual football competition organized by the Italian Football Federation and includes 20 teams. The one with the most points is awarded as "Italian champion" and participates in the Champions League. The three lowest ranked teams are relegated to Serie B. Serie A is hugely popular, with a high level of play and many talented players attracting the attention of football fans around the world.

48

The Italian football league consists of 4 professional series: Serie A (main division made up of 20 teams), Serie B (second division with 22 teams), Serie C (divided into 3 groups with 60 teams) and Serie D (fourth division with over 400 teams divided into 9 regional groups). Teams can earn promotion by moving up to a higher division, or risk relegation to a lower division depending on their performance.

49

Among all the seemingly unbelievable rules in the world of football, there is that of booking or sending off team members. This means that if they do not behave well, a coach, or any other member of the team's staff can be cautioned or sent off by the referee. This also applies even before the start of the game, in the event of misconduct.

50

One of the most amazing stadiums in the world is the stadium which is located a few kilometers away from Moscow in Russia. This stadium is located in the middle of an ancient forest, it is sheltered from the sun and has very tall trees, it is located in the Meshchersky park. The field would be at risk of invasion by Bears who live in the natural forest.

51

Cristiano Ronaldo was nicknamed "Cry Baby" when he was in school, due to his sensitivity. Whenever he passed the ball to his teammates and they didn't score, Cristiano cried. When he was 14, his emotionality caused him to react impulsively against his professor. Ronaldo threw a chair at him and this cost him a sound expulsion from the school. This fact did not stop Cristiano from becoming a professional footballer, on the contrary it facilitated him, as Cristiano better understood who he was and what he should have done in his life.

52

Lionel Messi's first professional contract was signed with FC Barcelona in 2000 when he was "only" 13 years old. Messi had joined the club's famed training academy, La Masia, as early as 8 years old, then continuing to progress through the club's youth teams. After impressing executives with his skills on the pitch, he was offered his first professional contract.

53

What is the goal at the Meazza? It is a goal scored following a personal action, in which the player, after having made various "numbers", presents himself in front of the goalkeeper and overcomes him with a final dribble entering with the ball at his foot and scoring into an empty net . This type of goal was named in honor of the champion Giuseppe Meazza who scored many goals in that way.

54

Cristiano Ronaldo grew up in a house in a poor hamlet of Funchal, Madeira, Portugal where he shared a room with his 3 brothers and sisters. Cristiano's parents were not wealthy and could not even afford to give him children's toys when their children were small. But to send Cristiano to play football, his mother made enormous sacrifices by working as a cook in restaurant kitchens, and Cristiano's father, on the other hand, worked hard as a gardener, this in order not to let their children lack for anything and to allow them a dignified life in any case. CR7 has always declared that he had a happy childhood and that his parents never let him lack for anything.

55

Lionel Messi was named a UNICEF ambassador in 2010. Messi has used his popularity and football star status for a noble purpose: to promote humanitarian rights and support programs for the development of underprivileged children around the world. As a UNICEF ambassador, Messi has participated in various campaigns and initiatives to raise public awareness of important issues, such as malnutrition, education and the defense of children's rights. He has also traveled to several countries to meet children benefiting from UNICEF awareness programs.

56

Among the most frequent injuries in the sport of football are muscle trauma, followed by blunt trauma, then knee and ankle sprains, and finally fractures. The incidence of injuries fluctuates between 9.5 and 48.7 every 1,000 hours of play. For example, in a squad of 25 players, in a professional team, there are on average about 2 injuries per season for each player - therefore about 50 injuries considering a calendar year.

57

Madeira Airport was renamed "Cristiano Ronaldo Airport" in 2017. Not only that, a statue has been placed in the airport hall in honor of him. However, according to some, the statue "was ugly" and bore no resemblance to Ronaldo's real face. Therefore it was subsequently replaced the following year in 2018 with a more precise representation, with a better aesthetic result. In addition, there are two other statues of Cristiano Ronaldo, one in Funchal, his hometown, and the other in Portugal.

58

Messi would love food and eat in general. What is his favorite dish? A variant of a dish with Italian origins. "La milanesa napolitana" – translated as "Milanesa alla Napoletana" - is an Argentine dish made with cheese, onions and tomatoes. In the dish there is also meat as a primary ingredient. The typical recipe consists of: slices of meat - usually beef - which are breaded and fried. The breading usually

59

The expression "Zona Cesarini" is used in football to indicate the final minutes of recovery. The expression refers to Renato Cesarini, a Juventus midfielder who scored numerous goals in the final minutes of matches in the first half of the 1930s.

60

40% of the world's football balls are produced in the city of Sialkot in Pakistan, not far from the borders with India. The city, with more than 1.5 million inhabitants, boasts over 140 ball factories, specializing in the production of high-quality football balls, all hand-made balls.

61

In 2012 Cristiano Ronaldo decided to face the Spanish sprinter Angel David Rodriguez in a zig-zag running competition. Rodriguez had the distinct advantage of running in a straight line. However, the match was lost by Ronaldo by very little. Ronaldo is known for his incredible speed, agility and athletic ability on the football field, skills that are uncommon, characteristics that have also allowed him to become one of the best footballers in the world ever.

62

In the semi-final of the 1938 World Cup, Giuseppe Meazza scored a goal almost in his underwear in front of the Brazilian goalkeeper Walter.

63

There is a type of football with motorcycles. It's called Motoball. The aim of the game is to score the opponent with a ball of 40 cm in diameter and weighing 1 kg, but in motion. The ball is carried forward holding it between the leg and the engine, according to the rules at least one pass is mandatory for each action.

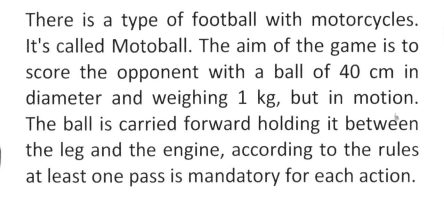

64

Lionel Messi allegedly suffered from a condition known as Growth Hormone Deficiency-when he was still a child. To cure that condition, Messi allegedly started subcutaneous treatment with synthetic growth hormone, which was given to him in the form of injections. This treatment allowed him to grow and develop normally, having no negative impact on his football career.

65

The 5 players with the most assists in football history are: 1st place. Lionel Messi. Argentinian and forward for Ligue 1 Paris Saint-Germain and captain of the Argentina national team, with 372 assists. Thomas Muller. 2nd place. Player of the Bunsedliga, Bayern Munich and the German national team, with 289 assists. 3rd place. Luis Alberto Suárez Dáz, professional football player for the Uruguayan national team and the Uruguayan Primera División Nacional club, with 277 assists. 4th place. Cristiano Ronaldo dos Santos Aveiro, Portuguese professional footballer. He plays for Premier League club Manchester United and is captain of the Portuguese national team and has 272 assists to his credit. 5th place. Angel Fabián Di Maria (born 14 February 1988) who competes for both the Argentina national team and Italian Serie A club Juventus. He has 268 assists to his credit.

66

Richard Wright, goalkeeper of the English national team (third goalkeeper at Euro 2000), in the warm-up of the 2006 FA Cup match between Everton and Chelsea was injured with a sign placed inside the same goal where he was training. Ironically, that sign read: "Please do not use this door as a heater. Use the smaller doors placed on the sides of the field...".

67

Ramalho, the Brazilian defender of Mainz, had a toothache one day, so he went to the dentist who gave him a pill to take to make the pain go away. Except that in fact, it was not a pill but a suppository. Ramalho took it orally, spending the next 3 days in bed with excruciating stomach pains.

68

"CR7" is the acronym of Cristiano Ronaldo, Portuguese footballer considered among the best of all time. Cosmos Redshift 7 is a very distant galaxy located about 12.8 billion light-years from Earth. It was discovered in 1996 and was the first galaxy to be identified at such a great distance, confirming the Big Bang theory. The galaxy was called "redshift 7" because its redshift (or redshift), caused by the expansion of the universe, is of the value of 7 units. This redshift has been used by researchers to determine the distance of the galaxy and to study the formation and evolution of the first galaxies in the universe. Another interesting theory about the name of the galaxy would be that Portuguese researchers named it "CR7" in honor of Cristiano Ronaldo.

69

Enrique Romero (former left back of Valencia, Mallorca, Deportivo and Betis) in 2003 during an away match in Pamplona had a close encounter with a viper on arrival at the airport, the viper bit him, making him spend a bad and unforgettable night in the hospital . After spending a whole day in hospital, he returned to the same airport where he had been bitten by the viper this time at departures, to finally return home happy with his companions. The match was off for him, but at least Enrique was healed!

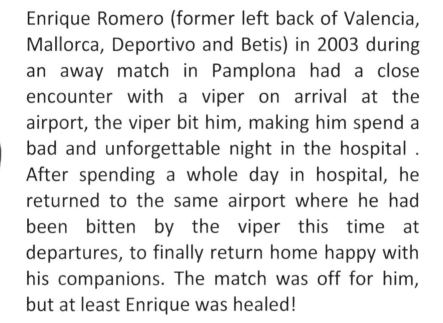

70

Fiorentina-Pistoiese on 27 October 1954 at the municipal stadium in Florence was interrupted due to "UFO sightings". There were 10,000 people present, most of those people saw sparkles falling from the sky. The game was resumed immediately after the interruption, concluding regularly with Fiorentina's victory 6-2 against Pistoiese.

71

Lionel Messi is the father of three sons: Thiago, Mateo and Ciro. Thiago was born in 2012, Mateo in 2015 and Ciro in 2018. Messi is very devoted to his children and often shares photos and stories of them on social media. As of 2021, Thiago has played as a midfielder for FC Barcelona's youth team. Like his father, Thiago also displays a natural talent for football.

72

The Ligue 1 record as longest-serving manager with the same club — but also overall — belongs to Guy Roux who coached Auxerre for 44 years. In this span of time Guy Roux managed to make Auxerre great, which climbed the French championship by also winning the title in '96.

73

In 2018 Cristiano Ronaldo was accused of tax evasion by the Spanish prosecutor risking prison. Ronaldo denied the allegations and accepted the payment of an administrative fine of 19 million euros to close the case.

74

The model Kinsey Wolanski, invaded the field at the 17th of the Champions final between Tottenham and Liverpool, with a black swimsuit and on her chest the advertisement of the adult website owned by her boyfriend Vitaly Zdorovetskiy.

75

Cristiano Ronaldo's father, José Dinis Aveiro, died in 2005 due to complications related to alcohol abuse. Ronaldo was very close to his father and has stated on several occasions that his death was one of the most difficult moments in his life. Despite his tragic loss, Ronaldo continued to honor his father's memory and use his success to help people in need, such as charities.

76

During a game of the Bolivian championship, a friendly police dog escaped from his master by stealing the ball and refusing to give it back. The dog ran madly across the field. Many were running after him - including the players - but the dog escaped by running faster than them. However, when they managed to stop him (now a tired dog with a ball that had already burst for a while) he finally rejoined his master.

77

Goalkeepers can hold the ball for a maximum of 6 seconds in their hands, after which they are obliged to put it back on the ground to play the ball with their feet, or to throw it outside the penalty area. If a goalkeeper holds the ball for more than 6 seconds in his hands, the referee can sanction the player with an offside foul or a free kick in favor of the opposing team. This rule was introduced to prevent goalkeepers from disrupting the normal flow of play.

78

The wind is not in favor of the goalkeepers, because it can deviate with unpredictable trajectories. For example, during the friendly match against Dynamo Kiev, the Israeli goalkeeper Makkabi Haifa kicked the ball out of his area, which unexpectedly came back to him as fast as a boomerang pushed by the force of the wind that was very strong that day, and under the astonished gaze of the goalkeeper the ball headed straight-straight into the empty goal. The goalkeeper was distant as he had come out of the area to kick him and he could do nothing to fix it. The referee awarded the own goal at that point.

79

In the match between Paris Saint-Germain and Reims of the 2019 French Ligue 1, Kylian Mbappé scored a goal with his hand. Mbappé was stretched out as if he wanted to block it and the action was striking. The scene went viral. The goal was not validated by the referee and Mbapè was booked.

80

Ronaldo is known for his poses. A famous pose is to place your hands on your hips, another typical pose is to show his abs. These poses have become an iconic gesture for the footballer after the goal, a way for him to show off his strength and determination. Furthermore, those gestures have helped to strengthen the image of him as a sex symbol.

81

During the match of March 17, 2007 against Espanyol, during a La Liga match, Lionel Messi scored a goal with his hand, imitating the famous "Hand of God" by Diego Maradona, an event that occurred during the 1986 World Cup. referee and linesman were on the other side and did not see the hand touch. Messi who was playing for Barcelona at the time simply turned a blind eye.

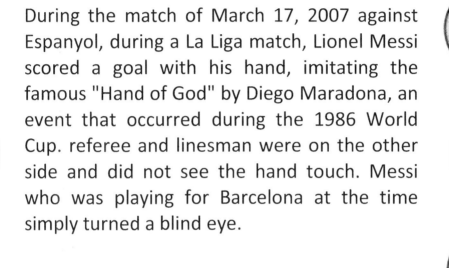

82

Paolo Dibala, an Argentine footballer, managed to take incredible free kicks with his left foot. For example, once in Spain he was given a very difficult punishment. The entire opposing team defended the goal. Some players even grabbed the crossbar. This did not prevent him with a surgical and non-linear trajectory from getting the ball into the net.

83

In one match, a footballer grabbed onto his opponent's shirt and was dragged over 15 meters. In football, holding an opponent's shirt is considered unfair behavior and can be punished with a penalty or a yellow or red card. However, it can happen that footballers resort to this unfair practice commonly.

84

During a clinical check-up, Cristiano Ronaldo was diagnosed with congenital tachycardia: a problem related to heartbeat dysfunctions, which could have proved fatal for him. Ronaldo thus had to undergo a delicate surgical operation to allow him to play football again. After the surgery, Ronaldo resumed his football activity normally and without consequences.

85

Yasper Schmeichel, Dutch goalkeeper, has gone viral due to memes imitating his pose leaning against the goal post during football matches. These memes depict Schmeichel in different funny and comical situations, such as sitting on the Christ the Redeemer statue in Rio de Janeiro or in other funny poses. These memes helped make Schmeichel a popular figure on social media and fueled his popularity among football fans and enthusiasts. The other funny poses depicted in these memes are goalkeeper Schmeichel sitting on a cloud, on a throne like a king, or on a stool like a bartender.

86

In football there is the possibility of scoring with the upper limbs. Only goalkeepers can do it, in case they manage to make a raise with their hands so hard that they are able to surprise the opposing team's goalkeeper. A particularly complex eventuality, but not impossible.

87

Cristiano Ronaldo with his 108 million dollars is in 3rd place immediately after Messi (2nd place) among the highest paid sportsmen in the world. Cristiano Ronaldo has generated a significant portion of his income through sponsorships and collaborations with companies. For example Nike is his main sponsor. Furthermore, he has signed sponsorship deals with other companies such as KFC and TAG Heuer.

Steven Charles McManaman is a former England midfielder. He is the strongest player ever among those who have played abroad. He is the only English footballer to have won the Champions League twice in a row with a foreign club. In his career he played for Liverpool, Real Madrid and Manchester City.

89

With 35 goals scored in 99 appearances, Radamel Falcao García Zárate, Colombian, born in 1986, is officially the best scorer in the history of the Colombian selection. He acquired the nickname "el tigre" for his lethality when he was in the penalty area, just like a tiger in the forest.

90

Zlatan Ibrahimović , Swedish footballer, striker for AC Milan and the Swedish national team (considered one of the best ever) earns 3383 euros per minute. The salary, on the other hand, is estimated at around 190 million euros, only in 2022.

91

If there is one operation that has upset the balance of world football, it is the transfer of Neymar da Silva Santos Júnior from PSG to Barcelona, an operation which cost a good 500 million between signing and wages. Neymar is considered one of the best footballers in the world and is compared to Pele.

92

Dan Magness, a 25-year-old Englishman, holds the dribble record: over 19 hours and 30 minutes of continuous dribbles with his feet, legs and head.

93

In 1888, the regulation was established for the first time which provided that the doors had to be equipped with a crossbar placed 2.43 meters from the ground. Until then, a common rope could be used.

94

The championships where the most goals are scored are: Spain is in 1st place with 2.90 goals per game, England is in 2nd with 2.86 goals per game, Italy is 3rd with 2.75 goals per game, Germany in 4th with 2.66 goals per game and France in 5th with 2.48 goals per game.

95

The championship where the least goals are scored is Ligue 2 (French second division) with 2.33 goals, followed by the Italian Serie C, where the average of goals is less than 2.20 per game.

96

The league with the most draws is the Spanish LaLiga2, in 1st place with 49 draws, tied with the Italian Serie B with 49 draws. In third place is the Portuguese Liga Portugal2 with 48 draws. In 4th, Holland tied with Switzerland and Denmark with 46 draws.

97

Cuban Erick Hernandez holds the record for dribbles, headballs, in the shortest possible time, 164 touches made in half a minute.

98

Vanigli, a former Italian defender and also a coach, committed a terrible foul on Totti in the 2006 Roma-Empoli match, in the 6th minute. Francesco Totti broke his fibula for a foot planted in the ground as a result of this foul. However, Vanigli declared his extraneousness to the facts "I took the insults, but I didn't even touch him".

99

Fifa attributes the title of top scorer to the Brazilian Pelé, author of 1,281 goals in his career. But not everyone agrees. For some, the record belongs to compatriot Arthur Friedenreich, with 1,329 goals, while others assign it to the Czech player Josef Bican, with 1,468 goals.

100

Although not officially provided for by the regulation, in recent years mainly in high-level competitions, at the discretion of the federations, the evanescent spray is used, a spray supplied to the referee, used as an indication to draw the limit line that the defensive barrier must not exceed , in fact, its foam disappears after a couple of minutes and is useful both for tracing the point of a free-kick and the limit point of the opposing team's barrier not to be crossed.

Printed in Great Britain
by Amazon

33665027R00061